Who Was
Henry Ford?

Who Was
Henry Ford?

by Michael Burgan

illustrated by Ted Hammond

Penguin Workshop

Dedicated to LBM, who has taught me many things
in such a short time—MB

To Mom—TH

PENGUIN WORKSHOP
An Imprint of Penguin Random House LLC, New York

Visit us online at www.penguinrandomhouse.com.

Library of Congress Control Number: 2014949844

ISBN 9780448479576   10 9 8 7 6 5 4 3 2

Part of the *What Is Science & Technology?* Boxed Set, ISBN 9780593090138

Contents

Contents

Who Was
Henry Ford?

As a young boy, Henry Ford had always been
fascinated by mechanical devices, such as watches
and wind-up toys. But nothing prepared him
for the sight he saw in 1876 on a Michigan dirt
road. Twelve-year-old Henry watched a small cart
roll along. The cart was carrying a
steam engine. Farmers used steam
engines to power farm machines,
and usually horses pulled these
carts from one place to
another. But the
owner of this
"road engine"
went one
step further.

By connecting a chain from the engine to the cart's wheels, the cart rolled down the path under its own power! Henry was amazed!

The farmer who owned the road engine moved to the side of the road to let the Fords' horse-drawn wagon pass. Instantly, Henry scrambled off the wagon and began asking the

farmer questions about his machine. The farmer explained how the engine worked and how he used its power to move the wagon. In that moment, Henry knew he would dedicate his life to building self-powered vehicles.

Eventually, Henry built the most famous car ever: the Model T.

From 1908 to 1927, the Ford Motor Company sold more than 15 million Model Ts around the world.

Henry Ford helped people move beyond the horse and the road engine toward a more modern world filled with fast and powerful cars.

Chapter 1
The Young Mechanic

Henry Ford was born July 30, 1863, on the Dearborn, Michigan, farm that was owned by his parents, William and Mary Ford. The couple had five more children over the next ten years: John, Margaret, Jane, William Jr., and Robert.

As a boy, Henry went to a one-room schoolhouse. There he showed an early interest in practical jokes. He was also good at solving math problems in his head. But Henry's greatest love was studying mechanical objects. When Henry was seven, a worker on the family farm took apart his watch to show the boy how it ran. Henry immediately began to learn everything he could about watches. He made his own tools from bits of metal he found around the house and explored the inside of any watch he could find.

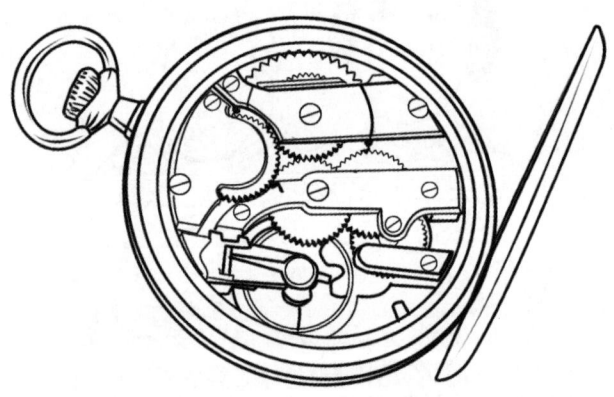

By this time, he had taught himself how
to repair broken watches. During school, he
sometimes worked on his classmates' watches,
hiding them behind a textbook as the other

students worked on their lessons. At home, Henry also loved to take apart wind-up toys. His younger brothers and sisters fought to keep their toys away from Henry. To Henry, toys were just "practice"—tiny machines to open up and study.

Henry's fascination with machines only grew. On trips to nearby Detroit with his father, Henry had seen steam engines on trains. A common source of power for machines of the day, steam engines burned coal or wood in a boiler to heat water until it created steam. The power of the expanding steam, held in a metal container called a cylinder, was then used to move some piece of machinery, like the wheels of a train. Steam trains could carry people long distances, but for most local travel, people relied on horses—or their own feet.

Back in Dearborn, Henry carried out a small experiment. With some friends, he built a miniature steam engine, but the device exploded,

burning down a nearby fence. Mr. Ford
didn't punish his son—he just told him
to be more careful in the future.

From then on, William let his son use a small shack on the farm as his workshop.

When Henry was twelve, the Ford family suffered a great loss. Mrs. Ford died shortly after giving birth to her seventh child. Sadly, the baby died, too. Henry later wrote, "I thought a great wrong had been done to me when my mother was taken." Henry always remembered his mother Mary as a loving and kind person. She taught him lessons that he remembered throughout his life—especially the importance of always working hard.

Just a few months later, Henry's life changed forever when he and his father took another trip to Detroit in July 1876. It was on this trip that Henry saw a self-powered road engine for the first time. The experience convinced him that he should be a mechanic and an inventor.

The life of a farmer was definitely not for Henry. To him, hauling firewood and plowing the fields was boring, tiresome work. So in 1879, when he was sixteen, Henry left school and Dearborn and moved to Detroit. He wanted to learn more about engines and manufacturing. With that knowledge, he could fulfill his dream of building a self-powered vehicle.

Chapter 2
The Appeal of Engines

In Detroit, Henry found a job at a company that made fire hydrants, pipes, and other items out of brass and iron. Henry learned how to run machines that made small metal parts. Needing money and full of youthful energy, he also took a second job at night repairing watches.

In his work, Henry met a number of skilled machinists and engineers. From them, he learned even more about steam engines. He also learned about a newer engine that ran on gas instead of steam, known today as the internal combustion engine. The gas was mixed with air and then lit to combust, or explode, inside a cylinder. This "explosion" moved a small metal piece called a piston, which could power a machine. Henry saw

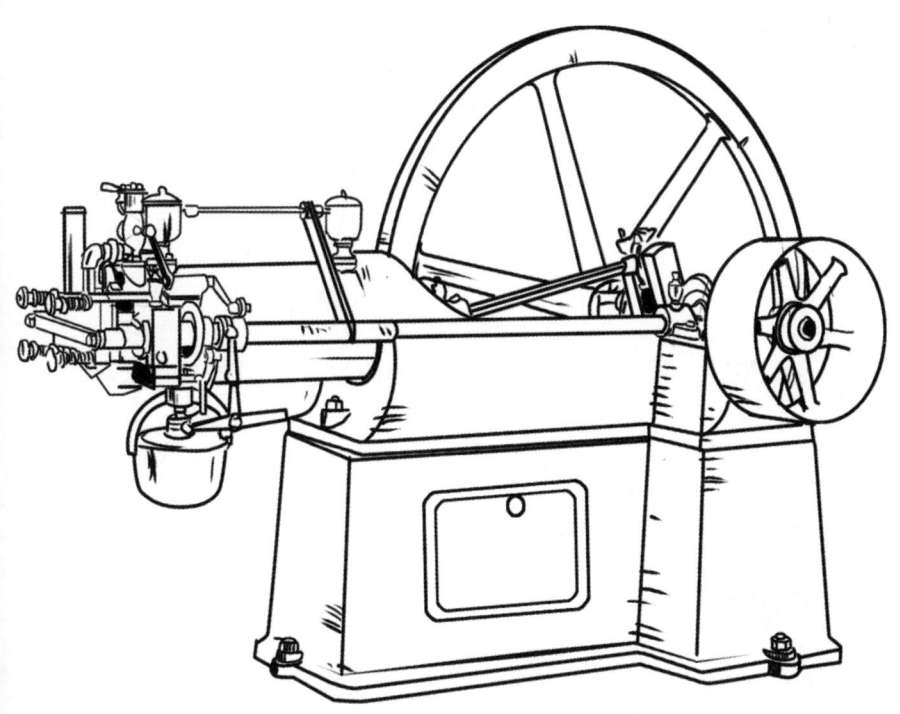

that a small engine like this could be used to move a vehicle forward.

Henry soon found a new job that actually brought him back to steam engines—and back to Dearborn. In 1882, a farmer named John Gleason hired him to visit local farms and charge people to use Gleason's steam engine to power wood choppers and farm equipment. Henry found great pleasure in keeping the engine running smoothly and driving the little vehicle across the countryside.

At the beginning of 1885, while attending a dance, Henry met Clara Bryant. He liked her immediately, and they began dating. Henry impressed Clara with a watch that he had made.

She liked that he was a serious person and willing to work hard. They were engaged in 1886 and married two years later. Henry built them a house on land his father owned.

In 1889, Henry went to Detroit to fix a gas engine. He returned home with a new idea: he wanted to build a gas-powered car. The first car with a gas engine had already been built in Germany in 1885 by Karl Benz. But Henry thought he could improve on the design. Hearing his idea, Clara was convinced Henry could do it. Ford nicknamed his wife "the Believer," because she never doubted his skills as an inventor. He wrote, "It was a very great thing to have my wife even more confident than I was."

In 1891, he and Clara moved to Detroit. There, he hoped to learn everything he could about electricity. Electricity, he believed, was the key for creating the explosion to power a gas engine. Henry got a job at the Edison Illuminating Company. At the time, Thomas Edison owned several companies that provided electricity to cities in the United States. Henry's main job was to fix the huge steam engines that generated electricity, and he did his job well.

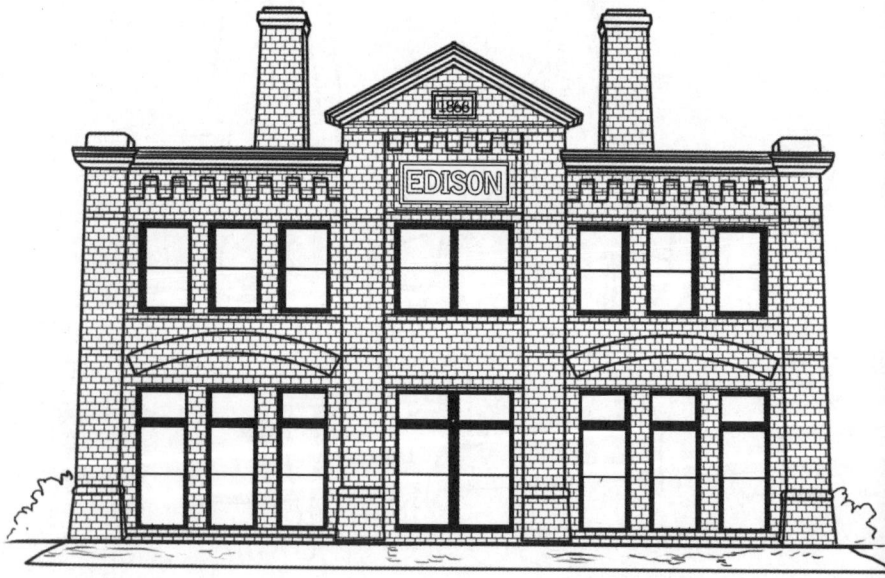

In 1893, Henry and Clara's only child was born—a boy they named Edsel, after one of Henry's old friends. Edsel was only a few weeks old when Henry carried out one of his great early experiments.

Henry had a workshop behind his house where he worked on building a gas engine in his spare time. On Christmas Eve, he brought the engine into the family kitchen to test it. It took two people to run and required electricity, which Ford did not have in his simple workshop. Clara willingly helped. She poured in the gas as Ford turned a metal wheel that got the piston moving. Then, with a spark from the house's electricity, air and fuel combusted, and the small engine began to run! Henry was happy, but not satisfied. "I didn't stop to play with it," he wrote. He wanted to build a bigger engine—one that could power a car.

Chapter 3
The First Ford Car

At the Edison Illuminating Company, Henry Ford had flexible hours. He had time to visit local machine shops and learn more about making metal parts. And he had time to develop his new engine in a small workshop he built outside the Edison company.

Fred Strauss was just one of the mechanics Ford recruited to help him build his first car. The two men got along well, and they often joked around. Ford made friends easily. Strauss said that "Henry had some kind of a 'magnet.' He could draw people to him."

Finally, on June 4, 1896, Ford was ready

to test his first vehicle. Ford called the vehicle a "buggy," but his official name for it was the Quadricycle. It certainly didn't look like a modern car. The driver sat on a short bench in the open cart and used a stick, instead of a wheel, to steer it. Its top speed was twenty miles per hour.

As he prepared for the car's first run, Henry realized he had a problem. The vehicle was too wide to fit through the doors of his workshop!

He had been working so hard to build his dream car, he never measured the front door! He took an ax and whacked at the bricks around the doorway to widen it. He then hopped in his buggy and headed down the streets of Detroit. The test ride was nearly perfect.

As he worked to develop his Quadricycle, Henry knew he was not alone. Inventors across America were racing to build automobiles. One had rumbled down the streets of Detroit just three months before. Like Henry's car, that one also had a gas engine. But other early autos relied on steam engines or power from a battery.

Henry was convinced that his design was the best. The gas engine gave his car more power than an electric car, and it was lighter than steam cars. The Quadricycle was light and strong at the same time. Henry liked simple things that would work well and last a long time.

Shortly after his first drive in the Quadricycle, the Edison Illuminating Company took Henry to New York for a convention. In New York, Henry explained his gas engine to the founder of the company—the great inventor Thomas Edison. He drew sketches to show how it worked. Edison's advice to Henry was "Keep on with your engine. If you can get what you are after, I can see a great future."

Those positive words thrilled Henry. Ford and Edison would eventually meet again and become close friends, sharing ideas and even vacationing together. Edison would praise Ford as a "natural mechanic" and a "natural businessman." But in the summer of 1896, Henry still had a long way to go before people would compare him to Edison.

THOMAS EDISON

THOMAS ALVA EDISON WAS BORN IN 1847 IN MILAN, OHIO.

HE RECEIVED HIS FIRST PATENT IN 1869 FOR A MACHINE THAT RECORDED VOTES. THE NEXT YEAR, EDISON MADE A SMALL FORTUNE SELLING A NEW MACHINE THAT DISPLAYED THE CHANGING PRICES OF STOCKS SOLD ON THE STOCK MARKET. HE THEN HAD ENOUGH MONEY TO SET UP A LABORATORY WHERE HE COULD CONTINUE TO EXPERIMENT AND INVENT. DURING THE 1870S, EDISON DEVELOPED THE PHONOGRAPH FOR RECORDING AND PLAYING MUSIC AND THE

PHONOGRAPH

FIRST PRACTICAL LIGHTBULB. THE SUCCESS OF THE BULB LED EDISON TO START HIS ILLUMINATING COMPANY, TO BRING ELECTRIC LIGHTS TO CITIES ACROSS AMERICA. ONE OF HIS LATER INVENTIONS WAS A MOVIE CAMERA THAT USED FILM TO RECORD IMAGES.

EDISON ALSO DESIGNED A BATTERY THAT FORD USED IN HIS CARS. EDISON WORKED IN MENLO PARK, NEW JERSEY, AND HE WAS OFTEN CALLED "THE WIZARD OF MENLO PARK." DURING HIS LIFETIME, EDISON RECEIVED MORE THAN ONE THOUSAND PATENTS FOR HIS INVENTIONS.

Back in Detroit, Henry improved the
Quadricycle. His second version was a little larger
and had a stronger frame. He sometimes drove
it to Dearborn with Clara and young Edsel.

On the first visit to the family farm, Margaret Ford saw how proud her brother and his wife were with their new "horseless carriage." She and the rest of the family got their first ride in a car that day.

By 1899, Henry was ready to leave the Edison Illuminating Company. He was ready to start his own company. He knew this was risky. As he later wrote, "Many wise people explained . . . [that the car] could never be more than a toy." But Clara supported him, and Ford was determined to bring his dream car to the world.

Chapter 4
Building a Company

Some of the wealthiest men in Detroit were now interested in horseless carriages. And, luckily for Henry, they were eager to help him start his own company. The investors included William H. Murphy, whose family had a made a fortune selling lumber, and William C. Maybury, the mayor of the city. With their help, Henry created the Detroit Automobile Company in August 1899.

He designed a new car model that was bigger than his second Quadricycle, but he was not quite happy with it. The company struggled as Henry made constant changes to the car and never produced one he could actually sell. His investors grew impatient and, after two short years, shut down the company. Although the

Detroit Automobile Company was out of business, Murphy and some other investors continued to give Henry money so he could develop new cars.

Henry was often away from home. He sometimes slept on a cot inside his workshop.

During 1901, Clara kept a diary noting how little she saw of her husband. One day, she saw him only because they happened to bump into each other on a streetcar! But as always, she knew how important Ford's work was to him.

Henry was busy that year designing and building a race car. He didn't care about racing himself, but many Americans did. Ford later wrote, "The public thought nothing of a car unless it made speed—unless it beat other racing cars."

THE FIRST RACE

THE FIRST AUTOMOBILE RACE TOOK PLACE IN AMERICA IN 1895. BROTHERS FRANK AND CHARLES DURYEA WANTED TO SHOW OFF THEIR GAS-POWERED CAR. THEY TOOK PART IN A RACE ON THANKSGIVING DAY, ON A COURSE THAT WENT FROM CHICAGO TO NEARBY EVANSTON AND BACK. FIVE CARS IN ADDITION TO THE DURYEAS' ENTERED THE RACE; TWO OF THEM WERE ELECTRIC, AND THREE OTHER GAS-POWERED CARS CAME FROM GERMANY. THE COURSE COVERED FIFTY-FOUR MILES, AND IT TOOK FRANK DURYEA MORE

THAN TEN HOURS TO FINISH IT. ALONG THE WAY
HE FACED ENGINE TROUBLE, HEAVY SNOW, AND
A TRAIN THAT BLOCKED HIS PATH FOR FOUR
MINUTES. BUT THE DURYEA VEHICLE WON THE
RACE, HITTING AN AVERAGE SPEED OF JUST OVER
SEVEN MILES PER HOUR. DURYEA NOTED HAPPILY
THAT HE AND HIS PASSENGER, ARTHUR WHITE,
NEVER HAD TO GET OUT AND PUSH THE CAR,
DESPITE ALL THE OBSTACLES!

Ford hoped that if he built a successful racer, people would see his skills as an engineer. They would come to know his name and be eager to buy the everyday cars he wanted to build for average Americans.

At the time, Alexander Winton of Cleveland
was the most famous carmaker in America. Part
of that fame came from winning automobile
races. In October 1901, Winton and Ford both
entered a race held at a track outside of Detroit.

Other drivers had planned to race, but mechanical problems kept them out. Only two cars rolled to the starting line.

Winton's car was bigger and more powerful than Ford's. Henry hoped he could compete, because his car was so much lighter. Henry's car was so basic, it didn't even have brakes! Each driver rode with a mechanic, who stood on a board attached to the outside of the car. Henry's mechanic, Spider Huff,

also added weight to the car so it wouldn't tip over during the sharp turns. Winton took an early lead, but the motor on his larger racer developed problems and he slowed down. As a newspaper reported afterward, "Mr. Ford shot by them as though they were standing still." In the stands, Clara watched with pride. The people around her stomped and cheered for her husband, the local automaker who beat the legendary Winton.

The win convinced William Murphy and other investors to start a second company for Ford. But once again, Henry was slow in developing a car he could sell. And he didn't like working for investors. He wanted to do things his own way. That desire for independence led him to leave the second company after only four months! He decided he would never take orders from anyone else ever again.

Around this same time, Tom Cooper, a professional bicycle racer, wanted to enter the

world of auto racing, and he asked Henry to build him one. Henry built another for himself. Both were almost ten feet long and had more power than anything Henry had designed before. When their engines roared, Henry said the sound was "enough to half kill a man."

Ford named the cars the Arrow and the 999.

FORD ARROW

When it came time to race one, Cooper chose another cyclist, Barney Oldfield, to drive it. Oldfield had never driven a car before, but he soon learned how to control the mammoth 999. In a race that October, Oldfield easily beat

Winton and two other drivers. Cooper owned the cars, but newspapers reported excitedly about the "Ford machines."

With his fame soaring, Henry once again looked to start a company that would build cars for everyday use. He found an investor named Alexander Malcomson who would let him run the company the way he wanted. In June 1903, the Ford Motor Company officially opened for business.

Chapter 5
The Model T

When the Ford Motor Company debuted the Model A in 1903, other Detroit automakers had already been selling cars. Ransom Olds built his early Oldsmobiles in the nation's first factory built solely to produce cars. Henry Leland,

RANSOM OLDS

who briefly worked with Henry, produced expensive cars under the Cadillac brand name. Henry used the power of advertising to convince Americans that his cheaper Model A was

HENRY LELAND

a better buy. As he had wanted to do for so long, Henry had finally built and sold a car that was well-made and simple to operate.

Early ads called the car "the most perfect machine on the market." The Model A sold well, and Henry soon moved his company to a bigger factory. He often walked among the mechanics, making sure that his plans were followed exactly. If an argument erupted between workers, he could easily calm everyone down. The employees at the Ford Motor Company respected Henry as an inventor and as a fair boss.

Henry sometimes brought Edsel to the plant;
the boy played outside as his father worked. At

age ten, Edsel received a Model A as a gift. Michigan didn't require driver's licenses then, since so few people had cars, and Edsel sometimes drove his mother to the store. In the winter, he thrilled his friends by towing their sleds down snowy streets!

FORD'S COMPETITORS

RANSOM OLDS AND HENRY LELAND WERE JUST TWO OF THE MEN WHO COMPETED WITH HENRY FORD IN THE EARLY DAYS OF AUTOMAKING. IN THE FIRST YEARS OF THE TWENTIETH CENTURY, DOZENS OF CAR COMPANIES WERE STARTED. MANY OF THEM SOON FAILED. ALBERT POPE BUILT CARS THAT RAN ON BATTERIES. ELECTRIC CARS, HOWEVER, WERE SLOW AND COULD NOT TRAVEL LONG DISTANCES. THE BROTHERS FRANCIS AND FREELAN STANLEY SOLD STEAM-POWERED CARS. ALTHOUGH THEY WERE FAST, THEIR ENGINES

1911
STANLEY STEAMER

NEEDED TIME TO WARM UP—AT LEAST TEN OR FIFTEEN MINUTES. GAS ENGINES STARTED RIGHT AWAY AND COULD CARRY CARS LONG DISTANCES. THEY BECAME THE PREFERRED POWER SOURCE FOR CARS. BY THE 1920S, THE FORD MOTOR COMPANY'S MAIN COMPETITION WAS CHEVROLET. FOUNDED IN 1911, IT WAS PART OF A LARGER AUTOMAKER, GENERAL MOTORS. FOR MANY YEARS, CHEVROLETS WERE THE SECOND MOST POPULAR CARS SOLD IN AMERICA—AFTER FORD'S.

Although the Model A was cheaper than many other cars, Henry was convinced he could build one that cost even less and was easier to drive and to repair. The car had to be light, too. A lighter car could use a smaller engine to produce fast speeds. Ford once said, "Excess weight kills any self-propelled vehicle."

Finally, in 1908, all of Ford's ideas on the ideal automobile came together. That year, he created the Model T. The car was larger than

the Model A. It sat higher above the road than most cars, so it could ride easily over bumps and out of holes. Although more cars were being made and sold, most people still relied on horses or walking for local transportation. Many roads were still just dirt horse paths, so being able to drive across unpaved roads was a plus. The basic Model T cost $850—not much more than the Model A. But the Model T was a much better car.

Henry soon decided that he would make and sell only the Model T. His ads promised drivers, "No man making a good salary will be unable to own one." Later ads stressed the pleasure owners would get while driving their Model Ts.

With a car, any driver could easily travel hundreds
of miles in a day. A car meant the freedom to
travel, and Henry believed everyone should have
that freedom.

The success of the Model T made Henry very
rich. He moved his family back to Dearborn,
where in 1914 he built a large home he called
Fair Lane. Henry liked to relax there by watching
birds and listening to Clara read aloud to him.

CAR CULTURE

BY BUILDING AND SELLING AFFORDABLE CARS, HENRY FORD NOT ONLY OFFERED PEOPLE A FREEDOM THEY HAD NEVER BEFORE KNOWN, HE ALSO HELPED SPUR THE GROWTH OF OTHER INDUSTRIES TIED TO THE CAR AND LIFE ON THE ROAD.

OTHER COMPANIES PRODUCED RUBBER TO MAKE TIRES, AND REFINED AND SOLD GASOLINE TO RUN THE CARS. CAR DEALERS SOLD THE CARS AND REPAIRED THEM WHEN THEY BROKE DOWN.

AS TOURISM BECAME MOTORIZED, PEOPLE WERE NOW ABLE TO VACATION TO PLACES ONCE VISITED ONLY BY THE WEALTHY, LIKE NATIONAL PARKS AND SEASIDE RESORTS. AS ROADS AND HIGHWAY SYSTEMS IMPROVED, ROADSIDE DINERS, CONVENIENCE STORES, GAS STATIONS, AND MOTELS SPRUNG UP TO SERVE THE INCREASING NUMBER OF AMERICANS ON THE MOVE.

CITY PLANNING GREW TO INCLUDE SUCH NECESSARY IDEAS AS SIDEWALKS AND DRIVE-THROUGH LANES FOR MANY BUSINESSES.

THE AUTOMOBILE CHANGED HOW AMERICANS LIVED. HENRY FORD—AND PARTICULARLY HIS MODEL T—PLAYED A HUGE ROLE IN MAKING THAT HAPPEN.

To entertain Edsel, now twenty-one, the house had its own bowling alley and golf course. Edsel had finished high school several years before, but instead of going to college, he worked at the Ford Motor Company to learn the family business.

He also had a talent for drawing, and he liked to design possible new models of Ford cars.

Even as he sold more Model Ts and made more money, Henry considered himself a simple person. He wasn't very concerned with his growing fortune. Workers reported seeing him take a crumpled piece of paper out of his pocket only to discover that it was a check for $68,000!

Henry had stuffed it there and then forgotten all about it! To Ford, making money didn't make a person successful. As he later wrote, "To do for the world more than the world does for you—that is success."

During the 1910s, Henry and his staff came up with new ways to make cars faster and cheaper at another new factory, called Highland Park. The main building at Highland Park was four stories tall and almost as a big as a football field.

Henry wanted to speed up production even more. As he later explained, "We began taking the work to the men instead of the men to the work."

This meant that, instead of having the workers walk around the factory to finish each detail of building a car, the car itself moved throughout the factory. A chain moved like a conveyor belt to

FORD MOTOR COMPAN

pull parts from one area of the factory to another. Workers did the same task over and over, such as adding a bolt to a part as it moved along. This process of moving parts through the plant and having workers continually do the same job was called an assembly line, and it greatly reduced the time it took to make a car. Ford workers used to take about twelve hours to make one chassis (the main body of a car). On the assembly line, the same job took just ninety minutes! Ford's new method was called mass production. One newspaper called it an "industrial marvel."

Ford produced more than sixty-five thousand Model Ts in 1912. All the other US auto companies combined made fewer cars than Ford! Chances were good that any car you spotted on the road was a Ford. All of them were painted black, because black paint dried faster than other colors. People claimed that Henry said buyers could have any color they wanted, "as long as it was black."

People began to use cars in many clever ways. Farmers reconnected the motors to different farm equipment and then used them to pump water or

cut hay. Some people even used their Model Ts to run washing machines! And by making changes to the car's body, the Model T was turned into a delivery truck, a taxi, or a police car. The Model T had several nicknames, such as "Tin Lizzie" and "flivver." People loved their Fords, and Henry wanted to sell even more of them.

In order to make cars available to more people, Henry decided to pay his workers more money. In 1914, Ford doubled the pay of many of his workers, from $2.50 to $5.00 per day. This

would allow them to easily afford the cars they made. He hoped they would be loyal to the company and work harder. Building cars by mass production was not exciting work. Some employees could not stay on the job for very long. Henry needed them at his factories and eager to work, and higher pay helped keep them there. He also believed that he had a duty to share some of the vast profits he was making from his cars. To many Americans, the $5 workday and the affordability of his car made Ford a hero.

Chapter 6
Growing Fame

Henry Ford enjoyed the attention he received as the world's most successful carmaker. He gave many interviews, and at times he even let reporters come with him on his vacations with his friend Thomas Edison. The two famous inventors, along with friends John Burroughs and Harvey Firestone (the tire manufacturer), became known as the Four Vagabonds.

They camped in the woods while still enjoying many comforts. In 1919, Ford brought along a special truck that was like a rolling kitchen, with a stove and refrigerator. A cook prepared their meals. And all four men slept on cots with a mattress and pillow. The Four Vagabonds, who were given that nickname because they liked to roam and

wander freely,
spent their time
exploring nature
and talking.
They also enjoyed
chopping wood
and climbing trees.
The reporters who
came along loved
seeing the famous
carmaker and
his friends
behaving like boys
at summer camp.

Being famous and having reporters around
much of the time meant that Henry's opinions
were widely published. In July 1914, war broke
out in Europe. Great Britain, France, and Russia
united to fight Germany and its allies. The British
and their allies wanted to stop Germany from

controlling large parts of Europe. Henry believed all war was wrong, and he began to speak out against the fighting in Europe, which eventually became known as World War I. He even disliked talk in America of preparing for war. He wrote, "Preparation for war can only end in war."

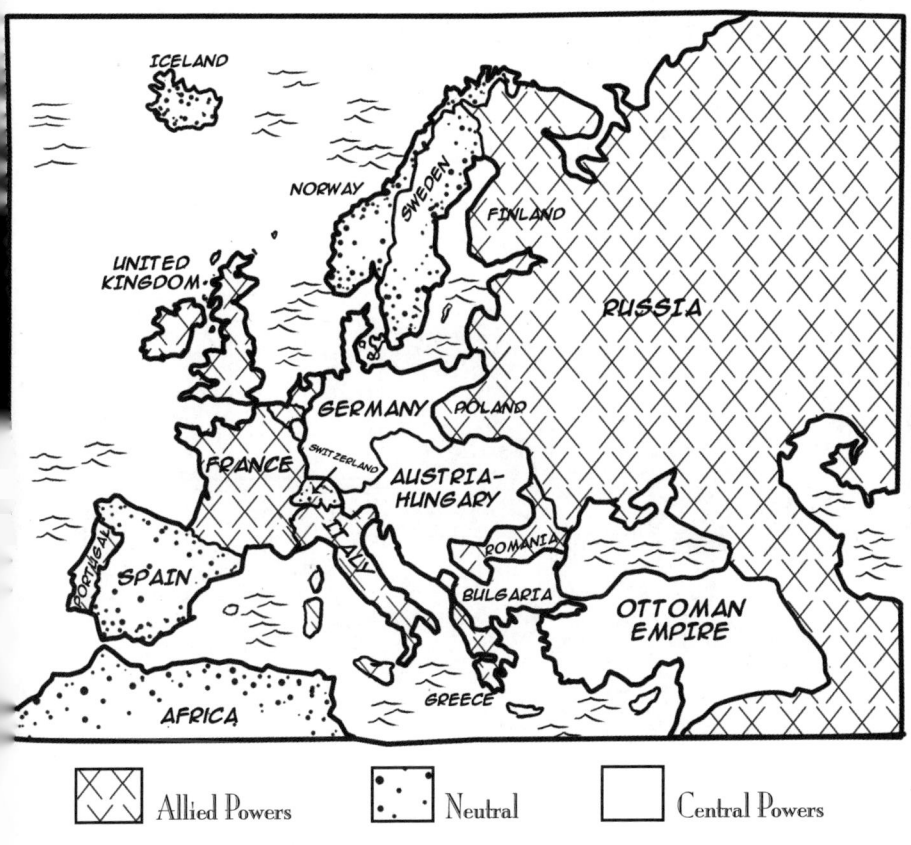

Allied Powers   Neutral   Central Powers

In 1916, some Americans who opposed the war and liked Henry's business skills hoped he would run for president. He said no, but two years later he accepted a request from President Woodrow Wilson to run for the US Senate in Michigan. Ford lost a close race. By 1918, the United States was also fighting World War I in Europe, and the Ford Motor Company was busy manufacturing Model Ts for military use and tractors for British farmers. Personally, though, Henry still opposed the war.

MODEL T
FIELD AMBULANCE

The war years saw a different member of the Ford family begin to play a major role in the Ford Motor Company. In 1916, Edsel took over as secretary of the board of directors, one of the top positions. He handled all the company's communications and some of its record keeping. Around this time, Edsel also married his high-school sweetheart, Eleanor Clay.

In 1917, they had a baby boy they named
Henry II. Their family grew to include two
more sons, Benson and William, and a daughter,
Josephine.

Eleanor came from a wealthy Detroit family,
and Edsel enjoyed spending time with her friends.
His father, however, had never really liked the

wealthy people of Detroit. He disapproved of
drinking alcohol, and he disapproved of people
who flaunted their money. Henry believed in
working hard and living a simple life. Edsel liked
to go to parties and museums and to golf and sail
boats. To Henry, Edsel wasn't tough enough to
run the Ford Motor Company.

Still, Edsel was his only child. In 1919, Henry named Edsel president of the company. Edsel soon realized that he was not really in charge. Henry would always be the one to make key decisions. Edsel rarely argued with his father because he respected him as a businessman. But he must have wondered if his father ever truly respected *him*. Charles Sorensen worked closely with Henry Ford for many years. He said that Ford's "greatest failure was his treatment of . . . Edsel."

Chapter 7
New Growth, New Challenges

It didn't take long for the Ford Motor Company to expand far beyond Michigan. As early as 1904, Ford made cars in Canada, and he began building Model Ts in England in 1911. Dealers sold Ford cars from Russia to Brazil and many points in between. People around the world recognized the Ford name.

During World War I, Ford began building a new plant outside Dearborn. It was named River Rouge, after a nearby river. But Henry wasn't

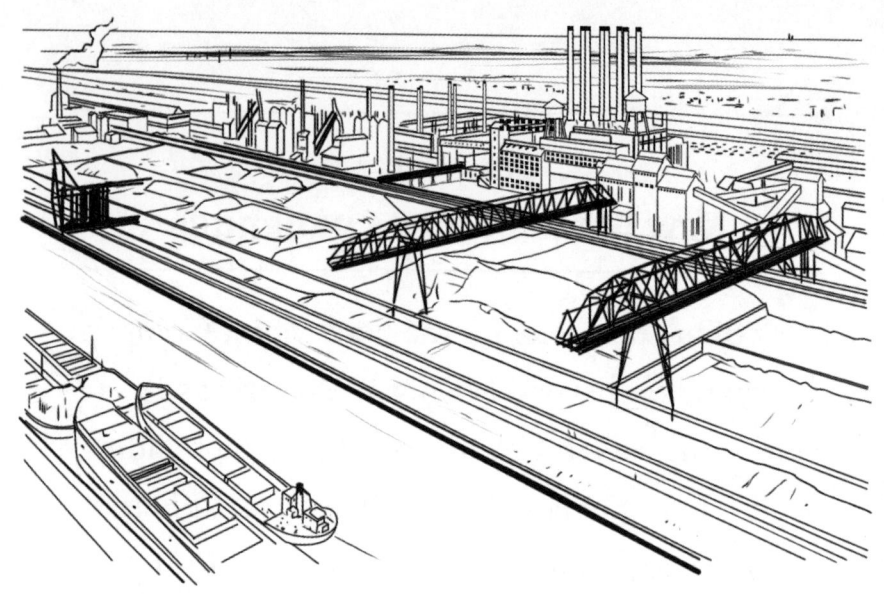

interested in just another factory. At River Rouge
he built a mini industrial city. Boats brought iron
ore and coal to the site so the company could
make its own steel. Other materials came by train
to a railway station built right into the plant.
Lumber was cut at a River Rouge sawmill. The
lumber, coal, and iron ore all came from land
that Henry owned. By controlling all parts of
production, including raw materials, and making

cars in huge numbers, Henry could continue to lower the cost of the Model T.

With his huge fortune, Henry also bought a radio station and a newspaper, which he used to promote and sell his cars. He also wanted to share his own personal and practical ideas for making the country better, just as he had made the car better.

Henry called the paper the *Dearborn Independent.* Each issue had one article that expressed his personal opinions. Henry often spoke out against bankers and investors; he believed they unfairly made money off of other peoples' hard

work, not by manufacturing or selling anything themselves. And some of his harshest words were directed at Jewish Americans. Articles in the

Dearborn Independent said that Jewish people controlled many banks and other industries and that they were weakening the United States. Henry did not write the articles himself, but he did approve them to run in his paper.

These hateful articles angered Jews and non-Jews alike. Former presidents Woodrow Wilson and William Howard Taft were among the people who spoke out against anti-Semitism—the hatred of Jews that Ford was showing. To some people, Henry's anti-Semitism reflected his lack of education. He had never trusted well-educated people—he preferred the simple farmers and mechanics he had grown up with. And Ford never claimed to be a genius. He was an inventor who knew how to make and sell cars. In 1927, when Henry finally realized he had upset Jewish Americans with the articles in the *Independent*, he made a public apology.

By that time, the man who had helped invent

the modern age of mass production was thinking more about the past. Henry longed for the simpler times of his childhood. He restored the house he had grown up in and several other older buildings. He began building a huge antique collection that included furniture, clothing, and household items from the eighteenth and nineteenth centuries. In 1928,

HENRY FORD'S RESTORED CHILDHOOD HOME

Henry began building the Henry Ford Museum a few miles from his Dearborn home to display his collections.

But Henry didn't just collect antiques. He found historic buildings and parts of buildings and moved them moved to Dearborn. One was the actual courthouse where Abraham Lincoln argued several legal cases when he was a young lawyer. Another was the workshop where Thomas Edison had created some of his greatest inventions. Although most of the building was not the original Menlo Park lab, Henry had every detail re-created at Greenfield Village, where he placed the buildings he found. The village, next

to his museum, grew to contain more than eighty historic American buildings.

While Henry focused more and more on the past, his son Edsel was trying to think ahead to the future. The Ford Motor Company had been selling only the Model T for more than ten years. Edsel's plan was to build a new car.

But Henry wasn't easily convinced. It took five long years before he finally agreed to build the new model. He played an active role in designing it, just as he had with his first cars. In May 1927, just as the 15 millionth Model T was rolling out the door at the old Highland Park factory, the Ford Motor Company announced its new car, which had the very same name as its original car: the Model A!

The new Model A had windshield wipers, an automatic starter, and other modern features. It was also more powerful than the Model T.

The Model A was an instant hit with American drivers. The car was barely more expensive than the Model T, and was a much better car. In 1929, production of the Model A peaked at more than 1.5 million cars. But then the Ford Motor Company, and the rest of the United States, hit a huge bump in the road—the Great Depression.

After World War I, farmers and many industries were producing more goods than people could buy. They were still growing and manufacturing at the same pace they had during the war. As a consequence, during the 1920s, companies began to fire and lay off workers in large numbers. Everyone who had lost their jobs could not continue to buy new things and pay their bills, so stores and banks went out of business. Henry Ford had to lay off workers, too, and he cut the salaries of others. By 1932, about 13 million Americans were out of work. The Great Depression sparked new interest in labor

unions that would help workers keep their jobs.

Labor unions were group of employees who sought to improve wages and working conditions. If factory owners refused their demands, the workers could threaten to strike—refuse to work. The owners disliked strikes; they would be forced to stop production, which meant they would have no products to sell. They also didn't want workers trying to tell them how to run their businesses. Unions fought for laws that helped all workers, such as shortening the workday to eight hours.

By the 1930s, workers in the auto industry wanted their own union, too. New laws, passed after the election of President Franklin D. Roosevelt in 1932, made it easier for workers to form unions. In 1935, the United Automobile Workers union (UAW) was formed.

Henry disliked labor unions and fought having them at his factories. He didn't want anyone—investors or workers—telling him how to run his business. By 1937, Henry had hired security men to guard the Ford plant. That May, Henry's guards

fought with men who tried to organize for the UAW there. Other workers acted as spies for Ford, reporting anyone who supported the unions. Ford angered many Americans with his harsh treatment of his employees during the Great

Depression. His support for workers by starting the $5 workday seemed long in the past. By 1941, other major automakers had allowed unions in their plants. Finally, Henry did, too. Although he loved the simple ways of the past, he realized that at times he could not always fight change.

Chapter 8
Last Years

As his company struggled through the Great
Depression and the rise of the unions, Henry Ford
spent more time working on Greenfield Village
and his museum. He also still found pleasure in
his boyhood hobby—fixing watches. Although
he was beginning to slow down physically, at age

seventy-five he continued to pursue new ideas. He experimented with different vegetables to see if they could be used in the auto industry. He thought he could help farmers by using their crops in new and creative ways. The chemists at Ford Motor had already made paints and plastics from soybeans. Henry later designed a car from the soybean-based plastic that was light and strong, but it was too expensive to actually build and sell to the average car buyer.

Meanwhile, Edsel Ford was designing and building new cars for the family company. Some were sold under the brand name of Lincoln. These cars were more expensive than Fords. In 1939, the brand Mercury appeared. As with the Model Ts, production of the first Mercury was international. It was built in such countries as Romania, Brazil, and Holland. Henry did not play much of a role in creating the Mercury, as he had suffered a stroke in 1938.

Two years after the Mercury appeared,

the United States was once again at war. On December 7, 1941, Japanese planes launched a surprise attack on the US naval base at Pearl Harbor, Hawaii. Soon Americans were battling Japan and its allies, Germany and Italy. Though Henry personally still opposed war, this time his company prepared to play a major role in arming the United States. Ford and other automakers stopped building cars so they could focus on making weapons. Ford built warplanes in a new factory south of Detroit called Willow Run. Almost nine thousand B-24 bomber planes were

built there during the war. The company used
the same kind of mass production methods it first
used on the Model T. The Ford Motor Company
also made airplane engines and Jeeps.

As World War II went on, Ford's health began to worsen. He suffered another stroke in 1941, and his mind was not as sharp as it once had been. He sometimes had trouble remembering the names of people he knew well. In 1942, Edsel developed

stomach cancer. Early in 1943, Edsel Ford decided that he was too sick and weak to battle his father anymore. He made plans to leave the company. But before he could resign, Edsel died.

Henry felt a tremendous loss with the death of his only child. He spoke tenderly about his son, sometimes crying because he had treated Edsel so harshly.

HENRY FORD II

With her son gone and Henry growing old, Clara Ford played a key role in the future of the Ford Motor Company. In June 1943, Henry once again took over as president of the company. Clara and Edsel's wife, Eleanor, suggested that Henry II run the company instead. But Henry was stubborn. He never had trusted anyone else to run his automobile empire, and so he resisted their idea. When Henry II finally did come work for the company, learning on his own how the company ran, his grandfather mostly ignored him.

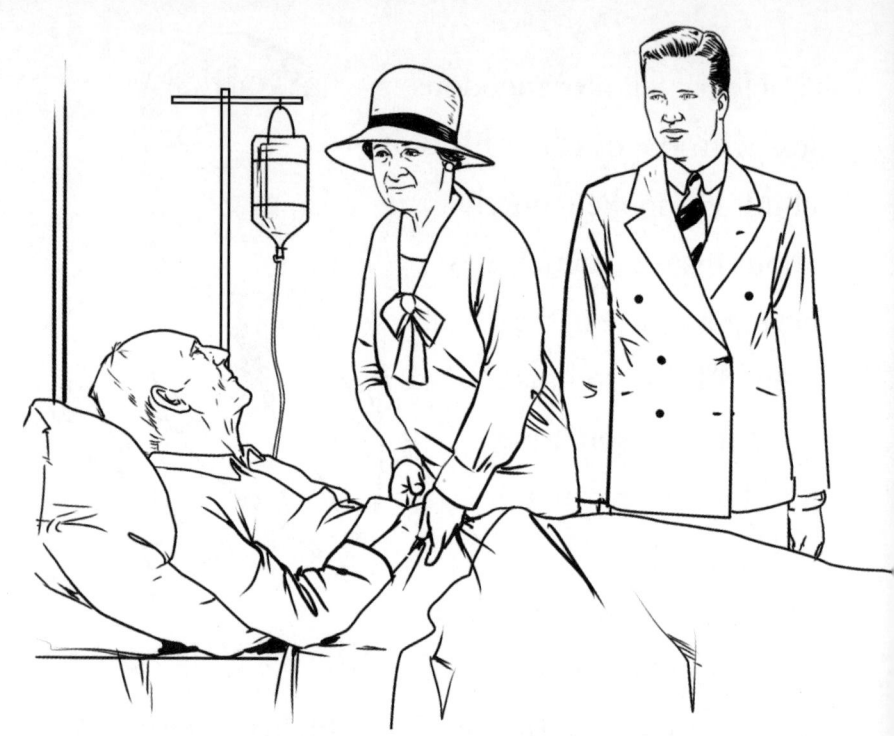

As World War II was coming to an end, Henry's health grew even worse. He suffered another stroke, and he forgot more and more things. Henry II went to visit his grandfather and said it was time for him to step down as head of the Ford Motor Company. Clara was there to support her grandson, and she said, "Henry, I think young Henry should take over." The elder

Ford still did not want to quit the company. After all, he had put almost his whole life into making and selling cars. But finally he agreed that Henry II should take over.

In 1945 Henry II became president of one of the largest companies in the world. It had 120,000 workers and was worth more than $1 billion. Soon it would begin making cars again, and it would find many eager buyers. World War II was over. People were ready to buy new homes and new cars. Henry II, and later his brother Benson, would keep Ford one of the world's major automakers.

Henry Ford lived his last few years quietly at home. On April 7, 1947, a blood vessel broke in Henry's brain, and he began to cough violently. The coughing fit caused severe bleeding in his brain, and Henry died. Clara was by his side, as she always had been. Two days later, 100,000 people came to Greenfield Village to honor him.

Americans cherished Henry Ford for all he had accomplished during his lifetime, including making the automobile part of their daily lives.

During the height of his fame, Ford wrote the value of people and ideas "is that of their ability to make the world a better place in which to live." The boy who loved engines became a man who truly made the world a better place to live.

TIMELINE OF HENRY FORD'S LIFE

1863 —— Henry Ford is born on July 30 in Dearborn, Michigan

1876 —— A passing steam-powered "road engine" sparks Ford's desire to build a self-powered vehicle

1888 —— Henry marries Clara Bryant

1893 —— The Fords have their only child, a son named Edsel; Henry tests his first successful gas engine

1896 —— Ford builds his first car, the Quadricycle

1903 —— Ford opens the Ford Motor Company

1908 —— Ford builds the Model T, which becomes the most popular car in the world

1914 —— Ford increases the pay of most of his workers to $5 a day

1916 —— Edsel Ford marries Eleanor Clay and they have their first child, Henry II, the next year

1919 —— Edsel Ford becomes president of the Ford Motor Company

1927 —— The last Model T is produced

1928 —— Ford begins building a museum to preserve items from American history

1942 —— The Willow Run factory opens, where Ford builds warplanes for the US government

1943 —— Edsel Ford dies

1945 —— Henry II becomes president of the Ford Motor Company

1947 —— Henry Ford dies at his home in Dearborn on April 7

TIMELINE OF THE WORLD

The Civil War, the battle between Northern and Southern states, begins in South Carolina — **1861**

The Civil War ends; President Abraham Lincoln is assassinated — **1865**

Thomas Edison receives a patent for the lightbulb — **1880**

German inventor Karl Benz receives a patent for the automobile — **1886**

The British ship *Titanic* hits an iceberg and sinks — **1912**

World War I begins — **1914**

US women gain the right to vote — **1920**

The mummy of King Tut is discovered in Egypt — **1922**

The United States enters the Great Depression, and soon millions of people are out of work — **1929**

President Franklin D. Roosevelt begins government programs collectively called the New Deal to ease the suffering caused by the Great Depression — **1933**

World War II starts in Europe — **1939**

World War II ends — **1945**

BIBLIOGRAPHY

* Abrams, Dennis. **The Invention of the Moving Assembly Line: A Revolution in Manufacturing**. New York: Chelsea House, 2011.

Brinkley, Douglas. **Wheels for the World: Henry Ford, His Company, and a Century of Progress**. New York: Viking, 2003.

Ford, Henry, with Samuel Crowther. **My Life and Work**. Available online at http://www.gutenberg.org/cache/epub/7213/pg7213.html.

* Gregory, Josh. **Henry Ford**. New York: Children's Press, 2013.

* Mitchell, Don. **Driven: A Photobiography of Henry Ford**. Washington, DC: National Geographic, 2010.

* Musolf, Nell. **The Story of Ford**. Mankato, MN: Creative Education, 2009.

* Raum, Elizabeth. **The History of the Car**. Chicago: Heinemann Library, 2008.

Snow, Richard. **I Invented the Modern Age: The Rise of Henry Ford**. New York: Scribner, 2013.

Watts, Steven. **The People's Tycoon: Henry Ford and the American Century**. New York: Alfred A. Knopf, 2005.

* Wright, David K. **The Story of Model T Fords**. Milwaukee, WI: Gareth Stevens Pub., 2002.

WEBSITES
Ford Motor Company
http://corporate.ford.com/

Henry Ford, The
http://www.thehenryford.org/

American Experience: Henry Ford
http://www.pbs.org/wgbh/americanexperience/films/ henryford/

* Books for young readers